MY

ADD

BRAIN

By
Sharon L Letson

Sascanda

Michigan ☘ California

ISBN: 979-8-9905086-4-4

Introduction

I wasn't diagnosed with Attention Deficit Disorder (ADD) until I was in my 40's. I was quite surprised at the diagnosis, because I really had no idea. I was resistant to the idea at first, because I just couldn't understand having a disorder and not being aware of it. Once I wrapped my head around it, I began recognizing the ways being ADD showed up in my life.

How could I have gone so long without being diagnosed? Part of it of course, had to do with the lack of knowledge about ADD when I was growing up. Also the psychiatrist told me that girls are very often undiagnosed or underdiagnosed because they have higher level coping skills than boys and very often don't have the physical hyperactivity component which makes ADD obvious to teachers.

At first, I wondered what having ADD meant and how that made me different, even though the psychiatrist pointed out some of the things I did that were related to having ADD. Since then I've learned more about how having this disorder affects me. I have probably learned more in the last year than I have in all the years prior, because a lot of people have been sharing on social media their own experiences with having ADD. I recognized myself in what they shared and that really helped me understand myself.

That's what led to this little booklet, as I began to think about how my brain works and the ways I cope with those differences, hopefully they don't trip me up too much. Recognizing that my brain works differently than some helps me understand myself. And to accept that it is ok for me to be who I am even if I operate on a different wavelength than others I know. It's ok that I don't always show up the way others think I should, and it gives me the vocabulary to explain to them why that is.

So, I started this journey by asking myself some questions. What are the ways that ADD shows up in my life? How do I cope with having ADD? How has having ADD caused misunderstandings with others? How can I help others understand the way my brain works?

ADD is Different for Everyone. There are a lot of people in my family who have ADD tendencies. Starting with the OG, our Dad. Of course he didn't know he had any kind of disorder, just that school did not come easy for him. Now that we know more about ADD it seems fairly obvious to the rest of us, but I doubt it's anything that he has ever given much thought to.

There is some discussion out there about whether ADD and these types of disorders are a result of nature or nurture. I personally believe it is both. Our brains are wired in a particular way, but our environment shapes the neurological connections.

Having so many family members who are affected by this disorder, leads me to believe there is a definite genetic component. I can also tell you that none of us are affected in exactly the same ways. There are definite similarities, but the degree to which a particular characteristic impacts a particular person can vary drastically.

The following list is MY list and isn't meant to diagnose any disorder, just to provide information which might be useful to someone trying to understand themselves or a family member. Another person's ADD may look different.

Distractibility

Distractibility has to be one of the most well-known ADD characteristics. When I was a kid, I daydreamed. It happened all the time at school. I'd be sitting there thinking of all kinds of interesting things, usually having something to do with recess, and all of a sudden realize that I had no idea what the teacher was talking about.

Even as an adult, I have difficulty focusing when someone else is talking, especially during staff meetings or presentations when I'm not specifically the person being spoken to or I find the topic uninteresting.

It also happens when I'm driving, especially when it's a familiar route. Some part of my brain must be paying attention to my driving, however I can suddenly realize I'm not sure where I'm at or whether or not I've missed my turn (I probably did).

I also get distracted when I have to do a set of tasks that are tedious such as a data entry task. It's excruciatingly boring for my brain to continue to focus on the list. So, I tend to jump around to make it more interesting.

That means I usually end up having a lot of different projects started and move from one to the other. Sometimes that means that I get too many things going and struggle to finish them.

I also struggle to finish my sentences. It's so odd to me that I can forget mid-thought what I was talking about, but it happens. And if the people I am speaking with don't remember the topic, it could be a while before we get back to it.

To me it feels like my brain is going faster than my mouth and when I'm relaying what's going on in my brain via my mouth, my brain keeps leaping ahead to different ideas and my mouth can't keep up.

How I cope with being easily distracted.
I have lists everywhere, for everything. That way I can refer to them if I need to remember something. And the process of writing the lists helps me remember, even if I don't look at the list. I even have to schedule birthday cards, so I don't forget to send them out on time.

I also create visual cues by placing items in places, so I'll see them and be reminded to do a particular task. For example, I will put my medication bottle on the table, so I remember to call to refill them when I'm close to running out. Or place the dirty clothes basket in my path so I remember to start the laundry.

If I'm running to town and have a number of errands to complete, I list the errands I need to do in order of the locations and assign each task to a finger. I then touch each finger and repeat them in order to myself, emphasizing how many errands there are.

If there are several errands I may create a mnemonic with the first letter of each word. For example, for the errands "prescription, post office and groceries" the initial letters of each word are p, p, g. I might repeat ppg to myself or create a word like ppig to help me remember the stops. If the list is too long, it may be easier to write the checklist and tick them off as each one is completed.

If I have something to do that is tedious or repetitive I will choose a set number to complete or do it for a specific amount of time before giving myself a break. Then I reward myself as needed for completing things. I can do a set of ten or work for ten minutes and my brain knows I can take a break when I'm done.

I usually only need a minute or two to reset my brain so I'm ready to take on another set. It feels good to pass the half-way point and know I'm closing in on completing the task.

Another coping mechanism I use is doing the same things in the same order, so I don't leave anything out. I can be standing at the sink in the bathroom in the morning and not remember if I took my medication or not within 5 minutes of when I should have taken it.

But if I do the same things in the same order I can see where I am in the sequence (yes, I already forgot). I also have a medicine reminder on my phone. Not to remind me to take it, but once I take it, I mark that I did, that way I can check when I am trying to remember if I took it or not.

And yes, probably staying focused when someone else is talking may be one of my worst things. If it is really important, I can help myself focus in two ways. One is by taking notes (don't start doodling!). I will probably never refer back to the notes I am keeping. They aren't necessary for any reason except to help me stay focused on what is being said.

The other way may sound silly, but it works for me. When someone is speaking to me, I repeat what they are saying in my head to make sure I am tracking with them and not getting distracted.

Before I knew I had ADD, I thought my difficulty focusing meant I was lazy. Now I know it just means that I hadn't developed the tools I needed to be more productive.

Easily Overwhelmed

Many people with ADD are easily overwhelmed which leads to things like anxiety, freezing (unable to function), and procrastination. These are all things I deal with.

This feeling of being overwhelmed comes from juggling too much information all at once. It's hard for me to focus on the task at hand because there are a lot of tasks I need to remember to do and all of them are vying for my attention.

For me, the resulting anxiety feels like having to write a 100 page paper and thinking about every single page at the same time. I obviously can't write the whole 100 pages all at once, but I start to worry that I can't get it done. And every moment I am obsessively thinking about all of those pages. I go to bed thinking about them, I dream about them, and I wake up thinking about them.

Then the anxiety leads to procrastination. The whole project is too big and overwhelming so it's easier to find something else more enjoyable to focus on, like scrolling through social media. Every time I think about what I need to do, I start to feel anxious. Feeling anxious doesn't feel good, so I do something that doesn't make me feel anxious.

Recently, I was trying to plan a vacation itinerary for my husband and myself. We had the flights and the hotel, but all the details had to be worked out. Were we going to park at the airport or take the shuttle? How were we going to get from the airport to our hotel when we landed? What sights did we want to see when we got there? I was definitely having anxiety trying to answer all of those questions and I procrastinated dealing with it.

If I have too much going on I freeze. It's like I can't function. This happens if there's too much chaos in my space. For me this happens when I travel from one place to another. When I get to the new location it takes me a few days to settle back into a routine and get a handle on everything. In the meantime, nothing really gets done. I just can't deal with any of it.

Something else I've noticed about myself is that I don't like change. I find my favorites and I stick with them. It's like the flip side of obsession is novelty which my ADD brain craves, but there is safety in sameness. I like my environment not to change and also to change in predictable ways.

Change, as the British say, "throws a spanner in the works." I recently described the anxiety I feel prior to travelling to the anticipation of stepping onto an escalator or a moving sidewalk. Step wrong and you can send yourself tumbling. Change is like stepping on the escalator. Once you make the transition, you'll be fine, but you have to be careful on that first step. Even if I'm looking forward to a change or I know it's a good thing I still get anxious about change.

How I handle being easily overwhelmed.
I keep my life very ordered and compartmentalized. Every day of the week has its specific tasks assigned to it. On Monday and Friday mornings I set aside time to do job #1, on Tuesdays and Thursdays I set aside time to do job #2. I will write on Wednesdays and Sundays and work on painting and marketing on Saturdays.

This uber organization of my schedule extends to which days I do the laundry, which days I plan to shower on, what time of day I am going to switch tasks, so that I remember to do something important, like cook a meal.

My bank account is like the old envelope system on steroids. Every amount is budgeted, and I get a daily update on the accounts we use most often.

I discovered that organizing things is calming to me. If I am anxious about anything I will find an organizing task and work on that. Completing the organization gives me such a sense of satisfaction and it eases the anxiety I was feeling, even if the anxiety was completely unrelated to what I was organizing. Sometimes I need to organize the space I'm in before I can start tackling tasks. Once the space is taken care of, I can look at the task list.

If a new task comes along, I assign it to a day and time when I will deal with it. I am giving my brain permission to not think about everything all at once and getting overwhelmed, because everything has its own time slot in my agenda. What day is it? Ok, I'm working on x today. I can think about y this afternoon or tomorrow.

That way I can push thoughts aside or create a note to think about it at the scheduled time. However, not being able to work on something on the day or at the time I assigned it to throws me off and can cause anxiety.

Anxiety. The way I dealt with our vacation itinerary was to push aside the anxiety it was causing me and to sit down with my husband to write down every detail that we already knew - flights, hotel check-in and out. Then I started filling in the details we didn't know.

When would we need to arrive at the airport? When would we need to leave the house? Does the shuttle run at that time? What was the difference in cost between parking our car in long-term parking versus taking the shuttle? What shuttle service would take us to and from our hotel? What were our options for activities once we got there?

I have amazingly detailed notes about our planned vacation. But it was the only way I could finally deal with it and make sure we got where we needed to go in a timely manner and had plans for when we got there. Once we did that, I felt so much better and actually was relaxed enough to get excited for our vacation for the first time since the anxiety took over.

The funny thing is, that my husband actually didn't do much except sit with me and listen to me as I worked it all out. Of course, he had some opinions about what activities we ultimately decided on, but he didn't know how to find what our choices were. Having him sit there was just calming for me as I worked through it and talked it through.

Procrastination. When it comes to writing academic papers (I have written plenty) the key for me is getting it started. Write an intro, create an outline, or just brainstorm my thoughts. Once I've done that, I can set it aside and come back to it later and pick up where I left off. The thoughts I already have written down will prompt new thoughts and I keep going until I at least have a draft of a paper that can be edited, put together and polished to be handed in.

Another way to tackle this is to list the steps needed to complete the project and then assign a deadline to each step. That way I don't need to think about the whole thing and can focus on the step I'm on. This method also helps me get other things done on time.

I can apply these two methods to the other

parts of my life that I might be procrastinating about. Get it started or list the steps needed to complete it and assign each of them a timeline.

Freeze. I noticed the freeze response the last time I came back from visiting my sister. I had been there for a month and a half and I had my routine worked out. Every day had its assigned agenda. Of course, I wasn't working on my agenda on the days I was traveling so after arriving home, my schedule was off plus I was in a different space.

Where I work on my daily agenda is also part of how I keep things compartmentalized. If the space I'm working in changes, or if the space has too much disorder in it, it can disrupt my ability to get things accomplished.

I had to organize my space and begin to reorganize my daily agenda to get things back on track. But the initial anxiety/freeze state kept me from being able to tackle it for a few days.

If I am overwhelmed, anxious, procrastinating or frozen, I have to find a way to organize myself, my tasks, or my space in order to be able to function again. I also give myself permission to not do everything that needs to be done at one time. I can do a piece of it and that's ok.

Obsessive

I heard an anecdote recently that a person with ADD needs to use 100% of their brain at all times, so if a task doesn't require 100% then having something else going on that can occupy the remaining percentage like music or a TV program on helps. The more brain focus the task requires the fewer extraneous distractions there can be.

I definitely find this true for myself. Focusing in heavy traffic requires silence, while normal driving requires music or listening to something streaming on my phone.

I've realized that if I don't have background noise on my brain will fill the silence. And sometimes the thoughts are obsessive or intrusive. If I'm half listening to a TV program it is helping me not go down one of a dozen ruminating rabbit holes.

The worst time for this is at night when I want my brain to shut off. For some people screen time before bed keeps them up. For me playing games or reading articles on my phone shifts my thinking away from whatever thing my brain has decided to ruminate on at the moment. I usually stay on my phone or tablet until I can't keep my eyes open anymore, because if I am not 100% ready to fall asleep my brain will start up again.

My obsessive thinking causes me to overthink about everything. I will over analyze interactions with others especially if I think I said something stupid, which happens too often because I spoke before I thought it through.

I realized a few years ago that I needed to work on my Emotional Intelligence. Basically, I lacked the awareness of when it was a good time to speak and not to speak. Just because I thought of something didn't mean it was a good time within the conversation to mention it. Maybe others were talking or maybe the conversation had moved on from what my comment pertained to.

This actually happened recently, when a conversation I wasn't a part of was happening at the table next to me among a group of people I knew. They were musing about the occurrence of redheadedness in families. Since we have a lot of redheads in our family I knew the answer, but I couldn't get their attention to interject my thought. When I finally did, it ended up feeling awkward and rude and they just looked at me funny and went back to their conversation.

Once when I was a teenager my sister and friends joked about me 'talking to the table'. I had thoughts and I was just speaking them out even though no one else was listening!

Of course, they laughed and I probably did too, but those kind of interactions led me to feel socially awkward and reluctant to speak as I was sure to say something out of place.

I think that's true for a lot of people with ADD. We realize we don't fit in the norm and so we try to adapt. Maybe we mask, pretend we're more like the others and mimic their behavior or maybe we shrink back and hide the parts of ourselves that feel awkward.

Another thing I can get obsessed with is with playing games. For example, my niece introduced me to Mine Craft and I played it solidly for a whole year before my obsession ran its course.

It is interesting that one of the hallmarks of ADD is distractibility and yet another facet is this obsessive thinking and the way we can hyperfocus on things. If I am mid-project I can get so caught up in what I'm doing that I'm not paying attention to things like being hungry, having to use the bathroom, or simply being too tired to keep going and think straight.

I'm much better at stopping myself now that I'm older, but there have been times when I pushed my limits and stayed at something way too long just because I was so hyper focused on it.

This tendency actually makes me quite good in a crisis. As long as I have something to focus on like a task list I can stay relatively calm. When my dad and husband's boat overturned while they were fishing and they ended up having to be rescued from the middle of Lake Erie we were frantic with worry because we didn't know what had happened to them. But everyone said the same thing to me afterward, that I was so calm.

I didn't feel calm, but I had this odd ability to compartmentalize my feelings and push them away. There was no need to think the worst while we had no confirmation that the worst had happened. I would not allow myself to think about it.

How do I cope with obsessive thinking?
Being aware that it is part of having ADD helps me accept it as part of who I am. I can let the obsessive thinking run its course, I can distract myself from whatever I am thinking about or I can take medication when necessary if I really need my brain to shut down.
Now that I know that I can get obsessive with games or other new fun things, if I find a new game to play and it feels like I'm being obsessive about it that the obsession will fade with time.

I give myself permission to obsess for a while because I know when I'm done, I'm done. I can also harness that energy and become hyper focused in order to get projects completed.

That might be fine with something as harmless as a game, but often it turns out that what I'm obsessed about is something negative or non-productive, so I have to find a way to distract myself.

I will turn on a movie, work on a puzzle, play a game, start a painting, or go for a walk or bike ride to give myself something else to think about. I've learned that if I sing a song my brain doesn't have the capacity to think about anything else.

Distracting myself is most difficult at night when I'm trying to wind down for sleep. Turning on sleep sounds or stories helps me keep my brain occupied until I am able to drift off to sleep. If I wake up during the night I often have to do the same thing to get myself back to sleep.

I also use white noise. I am hypersensitive to sound, or lack of sound so having the fan on is calming. I usually don't even have it pointed at me. I just need the noise.

If I really can't stop obsessive thinking about something I will take the medication I've been prescribed. It calms me enough to be able to fall asleep.

Hypersensitivity

I was an extremely sensitive child. Very shy and fearful. I was always being told I was too sensitive. Even as an adult if someone wanted to "talk to me" I assumed I did something wrong, or they were upset with me. But I never made a connection between my sensitivity and having ADD until recently.

However, according to WebMD.com there are studies that show you're more likely to be overly sensitive to rejection (Rejection Sensitive Disorder or RSD) if you have ADD.

People with RSD tend to feel rejected even when rejection isn't intended. Anything that isn't positive reinforcement would be viewed as rejection. If they aren't told specifically that they are wanted or accepted as they are, they believe that others don't like them or want them around.

Most people have an ability to cope with feelings of rejection but a person with RSD instead may feel anxious, depressed or maybe even angry.

I relate to that. I craved for anyone to say something nice about me. If I was in a performance at school or church, I assumed I wasn't any good unless I was specifically told I was amazing. Even if I received a compliment, I might not have believed it.

I struggled with anxiety and depression throughout the years. I tried medication a few times and have gone off and on, because I didn't care for the side effects. But I eventually came to terms with the fact that I do better on the medication than off. I am more emotionally stable and happy on medication.

There's another type of sensitivity that may have a connection to ADD. This is a hypersensitivity to touch, sights and sounds. I don't find this to be too much of a problem for me, but I am particular about the way fabric feels on my skin. I can't stand having any street lights or extra light coming into the bedroom when I'm trying to sleep. And I have a hard time ignoring the TV when it's on in the other room if I'm trying to relax.

Those things are easy to accommodate – black out curtains and white noise while I'm trying to sleep and buy clothes that feel comfortable.

For my emotional sensitivity I have benefitted from therapy over the years. I also use positive self-talk. I have learned that our brains believe what they hear and even if you are the one telling yourself positive things, your brain will believe you if you keep telling yourself those things.

Linear and Literal

I can see why I am a linear thinker. I live by checklists and organizational charts to keep myself on track. That makes sense for me as someone with ADD.

It does make writing fiction a challenge, because I tend to write from a point of this happened and next this happened and later that happened. I have to really think about the descriptive elements – the setting, the sights, sounds, smells. It doesn't come naturally to me. My mind fills in the blanks in between first, next, and last, so don't others think the same way?

I feel this is the reason I don't like disorganization. I have come home from being gone and gotten mad at my husband for having used the kitchen table as a repository for everything he had in his hand when he walked in the door during the time I was away.

As a family we like to play games, and we play a few card games that require a lot of cards. That means a lot of shuffling. My oldest sister likes just mixing the cards up in the middle of the table and having everyone choose the number that they need. She claims that they get mixed up enough, which they probably do, but for me it is just too chaotic.

When I play games on my phone and I play the same games in the same order every day. I tried playing them in a different order, but it really bothered me so I went back to doing it the same order.

I also find that I am a literal thinker. Not to the extent that I don't understand nuance or idomatic speech, but it takes some moments of analyzing for my brain to get there.

Again, I don't find these things to be too much of an issue for me. I think it is enough to be aware of it and be able to understand myself and explain it to others if it becomes an issue.

Landing The Plane

I had assigned writing to this morning but apparently, I didn't want to do it because I found 20 plus things to get distracted by on my way to opening my computer and actually starting to write.

My ADD brain loves to start things. I have a lot of thoughts swirling around and the excitement of getting the project going gives me the dopamine fix I crave.

But finishing projects can be like trudging through muddy quicksand. I refer to it as "slogging". It takes so much effort to even make a little bit of progress.

I have several writing projects started, and I'm ok with jumping from one to another because I get bored with the one and want to spark some excitement in my brain. But that also means I have several unfinished projects out there at the same time, all in various stages of completion. And sometimes finding the motivation to just push a project over the finish line is tough.

Apparently, those of use with ADD are a dopamine seeking bunch. Playing a game on my phone is more fun than reading a book because the dopamine hit is quicker. Listening to a story read to me via a platform like Audible is enjoyable because I can do something else while I'm listening and still get my hit of dopamine.

Anyway, back to finishing what I started. Getting a project off the ground is easier than landing the plane. Fortunately, or not so fortunately, I have a competing disorder (OCD?) where I hate to leave things unfinished.

I have a second Master's degree simply because I was only 2 classes away from completing it and I just couldn't let it stay unfinished. I love putting a check mark next to everything on my To-Do list. It's very satisfying.

So, I have managed to get myself back to my computer to try and wrap this up. In some cases this is just a willpower thing. Everything within me doesn't want to do it, but I know I need to. And once I get it started, I can usually bring it to a close.

My ADD, OCD(?) and Anxiety are considered disorders because they interfere with and affect my everyday life. Some people believe we are all neurodivergent in some way, but I disagree. If this was typical for everyone, those of us who are affected by it wouldn't feel so out of place or need to define it for ourselves as I've done here.

My ADD brain functions a certain way and I'm ok with that. I want to understand it better though because I have found that I miscommunicate often and some people have difficulty accepting my explanation of why I said or did a particular thing. They aren't as accepting of me as I am of myself and that can be hard to navigate and cause emotional distance.

My hope is that by sharing my own struggles with being ADD that it helps you identify, understand and cope with your own neurodivergent brain.

Having ADD means I'm a wonderfully messy and disorganized, distractible, procrastinating, CREATIVE person. Most of us with ADD brains are. And that's ok.

www.ingramcontent.com/pod-product-compliance
Lightning Source LLC
Chambersburg PA
CBHW060547030426
42337CB00021B/4471